PIG

HOROSCOPE
2023

Angeline A. Rubi and Alina A. Rubi

Introduction

*The Chinese calendar is
ancient and complex and
has never been simplified.
Many cultures replaced the
lunar calendar with the
calendar of the Sun.*

*The Chinese, Islamic and Hebrew calendars are
governed by the lunar phases. It is a complicated
system since they are not only governed by the
lunar cycles, but also include the solar cycle, that
of Jupiter and Saturn.*

*The Chinese consider universal energy to be
governed by balance. The concept of Yin and Yang
is the most important within that balance. Yin is
opposite to Yang and vice versa, but together they
reach total balance. This energy can be found in
everything that exists, the tangible and the
intangible.*

*The symbolism of Ying/Yang is divided into two
halves, one is black (Yin) and the other white
(Yang). Both parts are joined in the middle by an
ellipse that links them forming a curve. Its colors,
black and white, mean that duality exists, and that
for one to subsist, the other must undeniably exist.
Within the Yin is a Yang circle, which symbolizes*

5

that darkness always requires light. Within the Yang we find a Yin circle, showing that within the light we will always find darkness.

The ellipse that unites them means that everything flows, transforms, and evolves. If there is an imbalance of either of these two energies, Yin or Yang, our life is not balanced, as together they are strengthened. We must never think that one energy is superior to the other, both must concur equally.

Unfortunately, in our society there is a tendency to favor Yang energy, thinking that its characteristics are the most significant. By doing this we create a division between the spiritual and material planes, because by reducing the value of Yin energy we are less reflective thinking that susceptibility is something negative, because it implies fragility.

The same thing happens with darkness, not only do we avoid it, but we are afraid of it. Both energies are important. We can only be spiritual beings when there is a balance between Yin and Yang because you are not only light, but also darkness. It is a mistake to value and privilege the strong, or the action. We must appreciate and value the feminine, and sensitivity, since only in this way can we reach the true balance of our being, from a position of love and firmness.

In the signs of the Chinese zodiac the Yin and Yang energy are present, and they are the ones that will stipulate the characteristics of each animal, and the elements associated with them.

Yin energy is linked to the dark, cold, feminine, abstraction, the deep and the Moon. Yin signs are thoughtful, sensitive, and curious. They are the Ox, the Rabbit, the Snake, the Goat, the Rooster, and the Pig.

Yang energy is related to light, hot, superficiality, the Sun and logical thinking. They are impulsive, materialistic signs. They are the Rat, the Tiger, Dragon, Horse, Monkey and Dog.

The Yin and Yang energies are related to the elements, which in turn will be derived from the years in which they happen. Each element has Yin and Yang energy.

- *The years ending at number 0 their element is Metal, and they are related to Yang energy.*
- *The years ending at number 1 its element is Metal and are related to Yin energy.*
- *The years ending at number 2 its element is Water and are related to Yang energy.*
- *The years ending at number 3 its element is Water and are related to Yin energy.*

- *The years ending at number **4** its element is Wood and are related to Yang energy.*
- *The years ending at number **5** its element is Wood and are related to Yin energy.*
- *The years ending at number **6** its element is Fire, and they are related to Yang energy.*
- *The years ending in number **7** their element is Fire, and they are related to Yin energy.*
- *The years ending at number 8 its element is the Earth. and are related to Yang energy.*
- *The years ending at number **9** their element is the Earth. and are related to Yin energy.*

Origin of the Chinese Horoscope

The Chinese horoscope is a tradition of more than 5000 years and is based on the lunar years.

Legend has it that Buddha called all the animals, however, only twelve attended his convocation in the following order: the rat, the Ox, the Tiger, the Rabbit, the Dragon, the Snake, the Horse, the Goat, the Monkey, the rooster, the Dog, and the Pig.

Each animal received a year as a gift, forming the twelve-year cycle used by Chinese astrology. Therefore, each sign has a name of an animal, and each animal corresponds to one year.

Each animal was also assigned one of five elements that correspond to planetary energies:

- water (Mercury)
- metal (Venus)
- fire (Mars)

-   *wood (Jupiter)*
-   *earth (Saturn)*

The Chinese Horoscope expresses the analogy of cosmic energies with everyone. For that reason, the energy of each person is represented by one of the twelve animals that make up this zodiacal system.

Each animal and the energy that corresponds to you is determined by your date of birth. These energies define your behaviors, and how you perceive the world. For the Chinese, these signs symbolize the most remarkable particularities of our character. To properly understand the meaning of animals we must see them as spiritual symbols.

The Chinese Horoscope is not based on the solar cycle, on which the Western horoscope is based. It is based on the cycles of the Moon. Each lunar year has twelve new moons and every twelve years a thirteenth, therefore, a new year never coincides with the date of the previous year.

The twelve animals of the Chinese horoscope influence the life, luck and will of all human beings. These qualities do not manifest openly in daily life, but they are always present, acting in the form of hidden forces.

The Chinese twelve-year period is linked with the transit of the planet Jupiter, and each Chinese lunar year in Western astrology corresponds to the duration of Jupiter's transit through a zodiac sign. Jupiter is always in the sign of Western astrology that traditionally corresponds to the Chinese zodiac animal.

*Chinese Horoscope
Years from 1960 to 2031*

From 1960 to 1971

*1960 January 28 — 1961 February 14
Metal Rat*

*1961 February 15 — 1962 February 04
Metal Ox*

*1962 February 05 — 1963 January 24
Water Tiger*

*1963 January 25 — 1964 February 12
Water Rabbit*

*1964 February 13 — 1965 February 01
Dragon Wood*

*1965 February 02 — 1966 January 20
Wood Snake*

*1966 January 21 — 1967 February 08 Fire
Horse*

1967 January 09 — 1968 January 29 Goat of Fire

1968 January 30 — 1969 February 16 Earth Monkey

1969 February 17 — 1970 February 05 Earth Rooster

1970 February 06 — 1971 January 26 Metal Dog

1971 January 27 — 1972 February 14 Metal Pig

From 1972 to 1983

1972 February 15 — 1973 February 02 Water Rat

1973 February 03 — 1974 January 22 Water Ox

1974 January 23 — 1975 February 10 Wood Tiger

1975 February 11 — 1976 January 30 Wood Rabbit

1976 January 31 — 1977 February 17 Fire Dragon

1977 February 18 — 1978 February 06 Snake Fire

1978 February 07 — 1979 January 27 Earth Horse

1979 January 28 — 1980 February 15 Earth Goat

1980 February 16 — 1981 February 04 Metal Monkey

1981 February 05 — 1982 January 24 Metal Rooster

1982 January 25 — 1983 February 12
Water Dog

1983 February 13 — 1984 February 01
Water Pig

From 1984 to 1995

1984 February 02 — 1985 February 19
Wood Rat

1985 February 20 — 1986 February 08
Wood Ox

1986 February 09 — 1987 January 28 Fire
Tiger

1987 January 29 — 1988 February 16 Fire
Rabbit

1988 February 17 — 1989 February 05
Earth Dragon

1989 February 06 — 1990 January 26
Earth Snake

1990 January 27 — 1991 February 14
Metal Horse

1991 February 15 — 1992 February 03
Metal Goat

1992 February 04 — 1993 January 22
Water Monkey

1993 January 23 — 1994 February 09
Water Rooster

1994 February 10 — 1995 January 30
Wooden Dog

1995 January 31 — 1996 February 18
Wood Pig

From 1996 to 2007

1996 February 19 — 1997 February 06 Fire Rat

1997 February 07 — 1998 January 27 Fire Ox

1998 January 28 — 1999 February 15 Earth Tiger

1999 February 16 — 2000 February 04 Earth Rabbit

2000 February 05 — 2001 January 23 Metal Dragon

2001 January 24 — 2002 February 11 Metal Snake

2002 February 12 — 2003 January 31 Water Horse

2003 February 01 — 2004 January 21 Water Goat

2004 January 22 — 2005 February 8 Wood Monkey

2005 February 9 — 2006 January 28 Wooden Rooster

2006 January 29 — 2007 February 17 Fire Dog

2007 February 18 — 2008 February 6 Fire Pig

From 2008 to 2019

2008 February 7 — 2009 January 25 Earth Rat

2009 January 26 — 2010 February 13 Earth Ox

2010 February 14 — 2011 February 2 Metal Tiger

2011 February 3 — 2012 January 22 Metal Rabbit

2012 January 23 — 2013 February Water Dragon

2013 February 10 — 2014 January 30 Water Snake

2014 January 31 — 2015 February 18 Wood Horse

2015 February 19 — 2016 February 7 Wood Goat

2016 February 8 — 2017 January 27 Fire Monkey

2017 January 28 — 2018 February 15 Rooster of Fire

*2018 February 16 — 2019 February 4
Earth Dog*

*2019 February 5 — 2020 January 24 Earth
Pig*

From 2020 to 2031

2020 January 25 — 2021 February 11 Metal Rat

2021 February 12 — 2022 January 31 Metal Ox

2022 February 1 — 2023 January 21 Water Tiger

2023 January 22 — 2024 February 9 Water Rabbit

2024 February 10 — 2025 January 28 Wood Dragon

2025 January 29— 2026 February 16 Wood Snake

2026 February 17 — 2027 February 5 Horse of Fire

2027 February 6 — 2028 January 25 Goat of Fire

2028 January 26 — 2029 February 12 Monkey Earth

2029 February 13 — 2030 February 2 Earth Rooster

2030 February 3 — 2031 January 22 Metal Dog

2031 January 23 — 2032 February 10 Metal Pig

Your Ascendant according to the Chinese Horoscope.

Along with your Chinese zodiac sign, you also have an ascendant decided by your birth time. This animal will have a strong influence on the image you project towards others, and on the events of your life. You should also read the horoscope for the animal that represents your ascendant.

This sign of the ascendant symbolizes the energy that you can develop, and the characteristics, which, by striving, you can acquire. That is the reason sometimes we have different attributes to those related to our sign.

In the Chinese horoscope it is extremely easy to determine your ascendant, the only data you need is your time of birth.

Time of birth Ascendant animal

11.00 p. m. to 12.59 a. m. Rat

1.00 a.m. to 2.59 a.m. Ox

3.00 a. m. to 4.59 a. m. Tiger

5.00 a. m. to 6.59 a. m. Rabbit

7:00 a.m. to 8:59 a.m. Dragon

9:00 a.m. to 10:59 a.m. Snake

11:00 a.m. to 12:59 p.m. Horse

1.00 p. m. to 2.59 p. m. Goat

3.00 p. m. to 4.59 p. m. Monkey

5.00 p. m. to 6.59 p. m. Rooster

7.00 p. m. to 8.59 p. m. Dog

9.00 p.m. to 10. 59 p.m. Pig

Pig Ascendants

Pig Ascendant Tiger

They were born from 3 am to 5 am. They have a warrior nature. They are ambitious. They always succeed because they are persevering.

Pig Ascendant Rabbit

They were born from 5 am to 7 am. Super enthusiasts. Sociable in nature. Use your friendships to achieve your goals.

Pig Ascendant Dragon

They were born from 7 am to 9 am. One of the best lovers. It is detailed and romantic. He is lucky in gambling.

Pig Ascendant Snake

They were born from 9 am to 11 am. They are persevering, and they like to plan. Sometimes they are calculating.

Pig Ascendant Horse

They were born from 11 am to 1 pm. They have the quality of taking away their own to favor others. They can focus on their goals despite obstacles.

Pig Ascendant Goat

They were born from 1 pm to 3 pm. They are supportive and balanced. Sometimes they tend to get annoyed by the successes of others.

Pig Ascendant Monkey

They were born from 3 pm to 5 pm. They are smart and ambitious. Sometimes they comment on things they do not know. They do not know how to control their impulses.

Pig Ascendant Rooster

They were born from 5 pm to 7 pm. They live most of the time in a fantasy world. They make a lot of mistakes in their life because they do not pay attention to details.

Pig Ascendant Dog

They were born from 7 pm to 9 pm. They are affable so they have many friends. They are disciplined and organized.

Pig Ascendant Pig

They were born from 9 pm to 11 pm. They are happy, luck always smiles on them. They achieve their goals with ease. They are mature and responsible.

Chinese Element of the Year

2023: Water

This year pays tribute to water, Yin will be the element of the year. It symbolizes compassion, tranquility, discernment, and simplicity. Water stands for intuitive awakening; it is a call to purify our consciousness. This year a portal to meditation opens so that we can find inner peace. It is a sign to open our mind and heart, and it will be the only way we can receive the new.

Creativity is one of the main qualities that characterize this element, also adaptability. Without water the existence of any organism on planet earth is not possible, water is pure and crystalline, characteristics that meet those who own this element.

The element water in Chinese astrology represents wisdom, and the ability to adapt to any situation. Water, by nature, drains and moistens. It penetrates all the fissures, acquires any shape, is the best diluent and destroys everything in its path, destroying even the stones.

People who belong to the signs of the water element can moderately use the skills of others and easily remove all obstacles from their path. However, their purposes may be damaged by their lack of strength.

Those who belong to this element are impetuous, they go to the extreme of things, but they are also prone to analysis and adapt well to any circumstance. They are affable, tolerant and have a lot of intuition which allows them to predict events.

Meaning of the Elements in the Chinese Horoscope

Metal

People who were born in the years ending in 0 or 1 in the Chinese horoscope are categorized within the metal element. Metal, the material from which shields and swords are made, is the element that symbolizes firmness, and honesty, but also severity.

Metal is the element of autumn, season of collection and abundance. It is dual as the functions of its element, since in the form of liquid sword, and spoon feeds. Metal comes from the earth, is dominated by Fire, and transfigures wood.

The personality of these individuals belonging to the metal element tends to be strongly ambivalent. They perform better when they are alone because they do not have to answer to anyone.

They are determined, forgers of their destiny, stubborn, professional, and indifferent to any attempt at compromise.

Their freedom is paramount, and it is useless to try to pressure them, let alone help them, because they do not listen to anyone and do not accept intrusions and impediments. They choose to count only on themselves, and are not impressed by anyone, as they are powerful and capable of executing great jobs.

For them there are no difficulties that stop them, and even if a situation becomes untenable, they resist until the end. They are ambitious and calculating, love money, power, and success, and do not skimp on the means to achieve their purposes, even if it means breaking relationships.

They are designed for careers that empower them to express their element: jewelers, financiers, insurance of any kind, locksmiths, miners, surgeons, and for any context that allows them to distinguish themselves from others.

They can also succeed in professions connected to wood or paper. They will find those related to water beneficial, those related to land can cause conflicts and should move away from those related to the fire element.

*They are not interested in feelings, and they are not moved by the difficulties of others, to the point of manipulating them if they can gain any advantage from it. Those who suffer the consequences are specifically the people of the wood element since **it manipulates and subdues*** *them with frontal aggressions. However, people of the water element, as they are receptive receive an effective boost that benefits them. The only ones who can really bend them are the individuals who belong to the Fire element, as they master their callousness and severity with contagious emotion.*

Physically you can recognize a person of the metal element by their sad look and the anemic color of their face. It is fragile, prone to stress, and can be affected by changes in temperatures, and poor nutrition. That is why they should stimulate their appetite, emphasizing foods that have spicy ones.

The most favorable season for them is Autumn, and during it they can develop their full potential, although that does not mean that they should be overwhelmed or be stubborn. You should wear white clothes, and use as an amulet metal, and white quartz.

Metal is rigid and sharp; it is not afraid of danger. He is a kind of independent person, who, animated by greed, proceeds with perseverance, concentrates on success, plans, and hates spontaneity.

Once you adopt a path you do not change it. Despite their external insensitivity, people of this element radiate a magnetism that is perceived by all with whom they connect. However, to benefit from their abilities, they must learn to be less Dogmatic as this interferes with their relationships.

People born under the metal element should educate themselves, so that they can express their emotions. If you do not, you will feel your energies diminish.

Earth

People who were born in the years ending in numbers 8 or 9 belong to the earth element. To this element correspond the characteristics of firmness, persistence, and fecundity. Although in Chinese astrology, the Earth does not have a season of its own, it is related in the calendar to the last two or three weeks of the other seasons.

The Earth is the element that represents stability, and the tangible, but if there is an excess it transforms people into cautious, suspicious, and stubborn, restricting their initiatives and fantasies.

The person of the earth element is patient and humble, always working with constancy, without granting himself a moment of rejoicing or disorder.

He never tires and can be as busily and materialistic as he is naïve and prudent. His most unquestionable characteristic is his accentuated discouragement. He is too serious, loves to plan and direct, is horrified by coincidences, and, although he is intelligent and has an exceptional memory, he resents being resplendent to be resentful.

Indefatigably reflective, ambitious, and distressed, he is thus exposed to recharge the spleen, an organ related to this element, and which weakens when the person has a sharp mentality.

The person who belongs to this element cements personal relationships gradually but lasts for a long time. He is very devoted and defender in love, always ready to contract and fulfill his responsibilities, and although he is not demonstrative in his emotions, he is a shoulder that can always be counted on because he will be by your side in the moments you need it.

In their work they are serious and withdrawn, but also organized, and trustworthy. They are the right people to conduct business with fireproof morality, austerity, and honesty.

Their reasoning makes them insurmountable intermediaries in problems, contributing with their own practical and timely solutions. Is competent for professions that require dexterity, but do not involve taking initiatives, or leadership situations.

Although he is not an easy person to bear, because of how capricious and nostalgic he is, and because of his incompetence to be cheerful, he connects well with the metal element, to which he instills

stability, and with water, which he manages to contain and rule skillfully.
It usually has conflicts with the wood element, since, although it protects it, it sometimes also suffocates it, and with Fire, which drives it as much as it weakens it.

The earth element is related to the planet Saturn. He must be incredibly careful with him consuming sweets, something he loves since he is related to his element. You should always choose natural sweet and limit the use of white sugar as this destroys calcium from your bone system.

Its other weak point is the digestive system, which usually punishes you hard, for that reason you must maintain a light diet and comfortable digestion. It is recommended that you seek direct contact with Mother Earth, walking barefoot on the sand or in the field.

Its lucky color is yellow, and its quartz topaz, and citrine.

The Earth represents wealth, good sense, materialism, and security. These people are usually introspective which makes them have a great capacity for reasoning. The Earth is the vessel of life and these indelible seals those born under the influence of this element, since they are stable people to whom you can delegate.

The earth feeds on fire, generating a great energy that heats and melts the metal, can be subjected to water, and be consumed by wood.

To feel good, the person of the earth element needs material security, although it should be noted that he is industrious, formal, and organized. They can be reproached for being pretentious, but on their merits, they advance towards their goals slowly, obtaining stable results.

Fire

People who were born in the years ending in 6 or 7 correspond to the fire element. Passion, courage, and leadership belong to this element. The fire element is the element of the summer season, where everything bears fruit and reaches its consummation. It is related to the planet Mars, beneficial, but sometimes impulsive. It is excessively sterile and symbolizes the person who stands out, but also who mistreats others.

Combative, vain, and irritable, the person of this element goes from anger to jubilation unbridled.

Since childhood he has a personality of a leader, ambition is present in his life, he likes dangers, laughter, enthusiasm, and conflict. The difficulties instead of intimidating him encourage him to proceed, and in these cases, they undergo a violent metamorphosis.

These people were born to win, but they do not know how to admit it, because they do not manage to observe themselves and exploit their energies. Great in the military area, sports, and as bosses since others perish before their charisma. They know how to use the energies of the wood element, using their genius in their service, and induce in the people of the earth element the vital courage to keep moving forward.

People of the water element tend to extinguish their passion, and those of metal test them with a rigidity that drains their energy field.

The most easily damaged organ in these people is the heart, there is a possibility that they suffer tachycardia. In addition, they may suffer from the ears, and the intestine. They should wear brightly colored clothes, among which red prevails, and use quartz such as garnets and hematite as amulets. You should also use incense and candles.

Detached, enthusiastic and opportunistic, these charismatic people communicate well and focus on action.

Their selfishness and desire to succeed are incalculable and they rely only on their own views. They tend to neglect the details as they are sometimes stubborn and embark on goals that require intense work.

People born under the influence of the fire element are positive, always give their best and participate in everything they do with love and will. Their energies serve to sustain those who are in their environment and lack it.

Fire heats the hearth, allows us to prepare food. This element nourishes the earth through the ashes, feeds on dry firewood, that is, wood, its heat dominates the metal, that is, it makes it flexible, and can only be dominated by water.

A leader always has an abundance of the fire element and is always inclined to make quick decisions. He is attracted to unconventional ideas, is not afraid of danger, and is always on the move. It is important that you learn to have emotional intelligence, because arrogance can strengthen your selfishness and make it uncontrollable, specifically when you run into obstacles. This self-destructive style is outstanding in youth.

Success goes with the people of the fire element, but they must be cautious with instability and restlessness, which are the most common inadequacies of those born under fire. It is better to master these defects, so as not to be enslaved by them.

They should find a quiet place where they can be at peace, and meditation will also bring them balance.

The people of the fire element are tenacious, and lucrative.

 *Wood*

People who were born in the years ending in numbers 4 or 5 belong to the element wood. Wood is the element that symbolizes harmony, beauty, and creativity. They have an exceedingly high degree of self-confidence, and an iron will, which makes them the right people when it comes to fighting for a just cause.

Wood is related to the planet Jupiter, it is the most beneficial of the elements, symbol of permanence and knowledge. Adaptable, it folds comfortably, and has multiple uses, characterizing communicative, giving, and honest people.

People of the wood element are creative, and vital, but sometimes they are scattered and unable to find their way and fulfill their purposes.

They trust others to the point of innocence, and they like to rub shoulders with everyone, always discover new things to give and satisfy themselves. He is attracted to nature, and children, and gives priority to family.
Occasionally he tends to have impossible expectations, and they have the habit of belittling

his body, overdoing it with meals and letting himself be enveloped by passion and sensuality. They tend to choose pairs of the water element, of whom they absorb audacity and support, and of those of fire, whom they benefit by supplying them with their brilliant ideas.
It does not get along very well with the metal element, which ruins it without mercy.

The Wood element is recognized by the greenish color. These people should take care of their eyes.
With wood shelters are built, that is why it protects us. Wood coincides with the creativity of water, and thanks to that quality they understand and help others.

Those born under the wood element have internal conflicts to submit to the rules and traditions where the severe criterion is constantly in force.

This element nourishes water and, at the same time, is fuel for fire. Its energy is sucked in by the earth, and it is subjugated by metal.

The people of the wood element always get great triumphs, and they have a coveted structure.

Their vocations are versatile. They attach great importance to integrity, striving to find a permanent place in life. Believing in success, and his capacity for analysis give him the juncture to face the most complex problems without hesitation.

With incredible convincing power, they work in many areas, as they always have development and transformation as their purpose.

Their natural will helps them move forward, and they always find support and the necessary capital, since other people have their ability to transform ideas into wealth.

Their main obstacle is taking things to the extreme. Contained anger and courage negatively affect the energies of this element. Being close to the trees and touching them balances the wood element.

At work, individuals belonging to the wood element are neat, intelligent, and resourceful. In business activities, they are most fruitful when the work is in a team, and it is well structured.

No area of work related to its element is unfavorable, but those related to fire can affect it, and those related to metal will ruin them.

Water

The most insensitive and dark element, akin to winter, longevity, and the planet Mercury, is the ruler of communication and deep affections.

An individual of the water element is sensitive, but airtight. He is charitable, sentimental, and fragile, hates criticism and, for that reason, chooses to act undercover to protect himself.

He is cordial, eloquent and at the same time prudent, and knows how to overcome setbacks without boasting, with cunning, sagacity, and perseverance. In this way he achieves his goals, indirectly and silently, giving the feeling of being considerate and understanding.

Lacking energy means a problem for the water element, if it does not learn to level its impotence with the force that comes from reflection and communication with the deep areas of its being.

Panic is always the guiding cord of his dramatic life, often lived in darkness for fear of showing up and fighting.

On the professional level they are inhibited by competence, however, they perform well in clear and sheltered places, such as schools, bookstores, newsrooms or any place where communication, oral or written, is the primary mechanism, and in the company of peaceful colleagues who fit their personality, such as, for example, someone of the wood element, with whom the desire for wisdom coincides, or with metal, from whom he gets decision.

On the contrary, it does not adapt to the fire element, to those it extinguishes and discourages, nor to individuals who belong to the earth element, with whom it feels limited, conditioned, and hindered.

The color black is the one that favors them, but they should use it with moderation because it tends to discourage them.

The same goes for dark quartz, which attract luck, such as jet, onyx, and tourmaline. To make the best use of his qualities, without going to extremes, and not to disperse, the person of the water element should begin his plans in the winter.

In positive periods, the loving relationships of this element send tenderness, equanimity and caution, potentials that empower them to conduct themselves with the necessary sagacity to remedy the origin of their conflicts when they appear.

They have an incredible ability to reason, although their reserved, deep, and murky personality leads them to be prone to melancholy. They also present a lack of security and audacity.

Creativity is one of the main characteristics that represent this element, also adaptation, sweetness, piety, and sympathy. Without water there would be no living beings on earth, this element is pure and crystalline, qualities that those who belong to this element have.

People who belong to this element are affable and have a great command over others. They have an original intuition, which allows them to conquer quickly. Endurance and lucidity give them the opportunity to predict events.

They can perceive the faculties of others, inspire them effectively, but they are discreet and will not let others notice that they are using them.

Abuses with sodium or alkaloids, and prototypes of life that depart from common structures are very harmful to people born under the element of water.

. Respecting the hours of sleep, maintaining a relaxed mental and emotional health, and having

contact with water restores your harmony, and optimizes your energies.

Those who belong to a sign of the water element may have professions related to wood and fire and be successful, have jobs that relate to their own element, and decline careers, functions, and jobs that relate to the earth, as the earth subdues water.

Compatibility and
Incompatibility

Compatible Signs:

Rat – Dragon – Monkey.

They relate through their personalities who are highly active and friendly. All three are diligent, impatient, enthusiastic, and restless, and always have great aspirations in mind. They are full of ideas, have the stamina and courage needed to execute them, always supplying innovative, unexpected, surprising, and powerful solutions.

Tiger – Horse – Dog.

They are connected by the satisfaction they feel when they interact. They are united by modesty, dignity, honesty, and obstinate altruism. Insightful, cunning, and communicative, although a little violent and strict, they fight vigorously against inequalities, violence, and illegalities. These three signs never sell their consciousness.

Ox – Snake – Rooster.

These three signs are joined by their formality, wisdom, and the seriousness they achieve during their lives. Energetic, enterprising, and tireless, inflexible in their resolutions, they like to reconsider and plan calmly before obtaining commitments that they would regret later. Their lack is coldness, since for them reason must prevail over emotions.

Rabbit -Goat -Pig.

Three emotional signs that are also united by their creativity. Instinctive, susceptible, sensitive, and withdrawn, they easily adapt to their habitat, and as good profiteers they do not mind depending on others. His daily affirmations always carry the words implicit: perfection, covenant, and conformity.

Note: The opposite signs are opposing enemies:

Rat - Ox Horse - Tiger Goat - Monkey

Rabbit - Dragon Rooster - Snake Dog - Pig.

Pig

Characteristics

If the Pig were not so honest, it would retain more friendships, or it would not lose so many opportunities and suitable contacts. The Pig thinks that truth is above all, therefore, broken relationships do not worry him more than having a relationship whose basis is frankness.

The uncertainty that the Pig projects is the result of an enormous concern. They must meditate on everything a hundred times, and even when they decide on something, they doubt if having chosen another path would have been more convenient.

Despite all these uncertainties, when they decide, they have a lot of work to make a change and choose to continue the path with determination.

Pigs are complacent, condescending, and fair. His attitudes empower him for work, and jobs in which concentration is paramount.

In love he will be faithful, accommodating, and affable. Although they have a great sense of humor, and know how to enjoy life, in relationships they should not associate with very communicative individuals, or who are attracted to fun, since they like home life, and will prefer meetings with their close friends instead of meeting crowds.

Holder of great integrity, he is not dazzled by working on more than one thing at a time, but this does not limit him to going after the dynamic experiences of enjoyment, which in his wrong version could be his destruction.

The Pig is not attracted to being a boss, for that reason he is a loyal companion who will never compete to be the focus of attention, although sometimes he will be without considering it for his actions, becoming essential.

Charitable and honest, he is lucky and never lacks a faithful friendship that is determined to help him if he needs it. However, choose to provide rather than require.

Although it is very easy to outrage, he quickly renounces hostility because he chooses to be in harmony, which makes him complacent and resigned when it comes to cooperating and listening to any argument. He loves to do charitable works, he is not impressed by obligations, and it is as if he was born to fight against them.

His negative side, if he decides to expose it, is that he can be kind to take advantage of a certain situation and in this way without hesitation have anything as if it were his.

If he falls in love, he is devoted to his love and fidelity without asking for anything in return. He puts passion and happiness in all his actions, making his partner feel the navel of the world. He is very sensual, and does not know how to hide his emotions, nor refuse the claims of the person he loves, surrendering to dark passions.

The Pig is not a good leader and supervisor, and in turn he is irritated by being limited in his ambitions. That makes him selfish and useless. Their indestructible propensity to give expresses their great obligation to cooperate. He likes to live in the present and tries not to travel to the past, or anticipate the future, this being the reason he has a great power of rehabilitation and an iron determination in the face of the tribulations of everyday life.

Strongly meticulous, he does not rest if he stumbles upon formal disputes and although reasonable, he will feel the cause of the problem because he did not have the ability to maintain harmony.

The Rabbit and the Goat are his favorite accomplices because they share with him the need for serenity and harmony. The Tiger accompanies him on tortuous paths. The Rat, the Ox, the Horse, the Rooster, the Dog, and the Dragon share joyful opportunities with the Pig.

Another Pig is not a pleasant, nor entertaining association, but it will not work badly. The toughest oppositions are with the Snake and the Monkey, since he always loses with these two malicious little animals.

Characteristics of this Sign according to the Element

Pig

Metal Pig

The Metal Pig is friendly, and values loyalty very much. They are effective and daring. They stand out for their sense of humor. He is outgoing and his affection shows it openly. He possesses vision, entrepreneurial ideas, and an instinct for play, all of which contribute to his success in the business world. However, your confidence can also cause you problems, because sometimes you promise more than you can deliver, you miss significant details that must be censored, and you can overestimate the potential of an idea.

The Metal Pig possesses an excellent power of concentration and likes to study or think deeply in solitude. He is thorough and rational, with the ability to get to the center of any discussion and can quickly see weaknesses in other people's logic.

This Pig enjoys working on problems that others consider very boring, iterative, and technical. He has a tendency to devote himself to some area of knowledge and to be enraptured in all the details of that area, sometimes ignoring that few people share his personal interest, especially at his level.

He has ties to his past, the place where he was born, and family traditions. Really, it is not possible for him to break with the habits and roles learned during his childhood. The connection with his mother is strong, and this Pig seeks affection and protection in his partner and other members of his family.

Water Pig

The Water Pig does not express itself easily, even though it has much to declare. His mind tends to wander, and he finds it difficult to study very realistic subjects that do not have much color or idealism. Your perception and the first emotions you feel are likely to be accurate, with a tendency to rely on this ability to make decisions. He has an expressive predisposition, and the ability to reach out to others in a friendly way.

His emotional greatness, and lack of pettiness is greatly admired in his circle of friends, and they often seek him out for help or advice. He is always willing to overlook the faults of others and sometimes his hand goes out in compassion.

He has an inner attitude and balance that allows him to proceed efficiently during traumas and emotional stress. He maintains objectivity around emotionally charged issues, often to the distress of others who would long for him to react more forcefully.

This Pig experiences strong attractions of great emotional and sexual potency, and may feel that he has little control over his desires. He has a pervasive need for love, and can be emotionally insatiable. Her love life is enthusiastic, turbulent, and painful. Jealousy, power struggles, and manipulation can become conflict zones in your relationships.

He faces many challenges, and many obstacles in pursuing his purposes and desires. These setbacks frequently occur to him because this Pig has done things in a hurry or tried to work according to his will without caring about the impact on others.

Wood Pig

The Wood Pig takes his goals seriously and knows that keeping working is the only way to achieve them. Persistent effort, and concentration on a single goal are the ways you achieve your goals in life.

He stoically faces difficulties and will fight patiently through problems. He knows inside that he can only depend on himself, that everything is on his back, and he can be very inflexible in instilling discipline, as he has high expectations.

This Pig is often limited, doubting his own ability. He feels that he encounters great resistance when trying to be assertive, and this can be very frustrating. However, he has the capacity to be consistent, and determination to overcome all obstacles.

Courtesy, good manners and proper behavior are particularly important to this Pig. His calm, objective attitude is, to others, the first thing, and although he is extremely helpful, he does not radiate much sympathy, so that others may not see that side of his temperament immediately.

He can look methodical and objective and even more conservative than he is at heart. He is the type of person to turn to for advice, or to ask for an opinion without prejudice, but not to seek emotional support.

The Wood Pig is very practical and wants to see tangible results from his efforts, as he is not one to weave crazy dreams. All of his dreams have to do with material achievements, and security, as he has a great love for the physical world and wants to enjoy it to the fullest.

Fire Pig

The Fire Pig has three main flaws, one of which is his stubborn stubbornness. The second is his lack of interest in deviating from his comfortable routine, and the third is his tendency to devalue the imaginative, the speculative, and the fanciful, in other words, the inability to play with ideas and possibilities, and to open his mind to the new.

When the Fire Pig decides what he wants to do, he does it with tenacity, and if necessary, he will sacrifice himself to reach his deep convictions. This trait is not very common, and, in fact, tends to make you feel a little out of place in relation to others.

He takes things very formally and has a tendency to be a little fanatical, though probably not openly, so others may not know how much the things that are important affect him and drive him. He has a resolute will and willingness to fight to achieve things that have true meaning, rather than following an easier, but less meaningful course in life.

He doubts his intelligence and mental abilities, and works very hard with his studies in order to remedy this. He is often profoundly serious and disinterested in trivial conversations, and general conversations are probably somewhat difficult for him.

Earth Pigs

Earth Pigs cannot tolerate trifles of any kind and have a tendency to exaggerate. In addition, they have a beautiful sense of dramatization. The desire to receive personal recognition, and the need to do something that you are really proud of, motivate you strongly. He has an unusual ability to have fun and be mischievous.

He is an entrepreneur, and has a great interest in succeeding in a big way. He is always looking for new opportunities and businesses, and is willing to run risks if he senses that he is behind a triumph. No matter what he achieves, he never seems to be completely satisfied. He always feels he can do more and sets his sights on another goal.

You feel frustrated in limited circumstances, and would abandon scenarios of relative success and security if they do not offer you the potential to expand and grow in the future. He likes to keep pushing his limits, until he sees how far he can go.

This Pig tends to lose patience very easily, especially with undecided people. He needs to see immediate results, and he can't stand waiting, which can lead him to rush his decisions. You have to learn to think before you speak or act, because many times you will act on impulse complicating the situation or expose yourself to dangerous situations.

Ritual to Start the Chinese New Year 2023

The Chinese New Year should be received with joy, music, and a splendid family meal. It is a period to celebrate and focus on luck and prosperity for the coming year. You should wear new clothes because this symbolizes a new beginning. A resonant color, such as red, which usually is harmony, good luck, and well-being, is great for this day. Avoid wearing black or white during the New Year's Eve, as these are the colors that people usually wear for funerals.

Doing a cleanse to be prepared for the Chinese New Year, in the form of a ritual, is beneficial. With this cleaning we try to ward off evil spirits that could be hiding in the corners of the house. Usually, people change furniture or move it, touch up the paint on their home, repair what is damaged, and wash windows with plenty of water.

Ritual for Energy Purification

That same afternoon, before the year begins, you should clean your house, open all the windows so that it is ventilated, and put white and yellow flowers in all common areas of your home. Specifically at the entrance you must place cinnamon, sandalwood, eucalyptus or lavender incense, or an incense of Palo Santo, White Sage, or Vanilla.

You must smoke the house well. Sahumar is the action of creating smoke, usually using incense, to aromatize the environment, and to use it as an instrument of purification and cleaning. Their particularity is that they expel a pleasant fragrance, to which relaxing properties are attributed. Many people use incense burners with the aim of changing the energetic vibrations of their home.

If you have an incense that you are going to pass through the whole house, remember that you must make circular movements to the right. If you intend to purify a personal area, you should start with your own body starting from your feet to the head, and then return to the heart part, always making light circles.

As this is the year of the Rabbit it is advisable to have a couple of metal or wood Rabbits in your home, and if you have the possibility, some glass as these is the element of the year: water.

If you do not have that opportunity then you can symbolize it with images, portraits, or figures. Consider it a lucky talisman, because in the end the Rabbit strives to safeguard prosperity. It will bring a lot of wealth into your home.

Another recommendation for 2023 is that you paint some of the walls of your home celestial blue.

This color is one of the colors of prosperity for this new year. Be careful about stuffing your house with blue, you should never forget that maintaining balance is the most important thing. If you overdo it in blue, you will be attracting discouragement or apathy.

Another alternative or option is to take it with you, in the form of a bracelet, hanging earrings, pendulums, a ring, keychain or a talisman inside your pocket, or wallet. If you have both Rabbit and water, this will form an association of wealth, shelter and good luck in your life, in your home or office. Always keep in mind that everything is accompanied by perseverance and effort.

If you can buy plants like Basil that has a great capacity to generate abundance, in addition to its power to ward off and transmute bad vibrations, you will not regret it. Having Jasmine would be another good option, your home will always be aromatized and with good vibrations. You should have fresh jasmine in your house whenever you have the possibility, but the most vital thing is that on the first day of the Chinese year they are in any corner of your home.

Predictions for 2023

Pig

After a long period where everything was confusion in the life of the Pig, everything begins to take shape in 2023. It will be a year of affirmation in all areas, and they will receive many rewards for the patience they have shown. You cannot give up right now, now you have to trust yourself more than ever because this is the key to success.

This year 2023 is very good for love, you can start stable relationships, and married life will be very pleasant. You should be careful with your words because they can hurt the people around you, including people who have a particular meaning in your life.

There are chances that you will remain single, if you do not have a partner. Throughout the year it is likely that there will be no major changes in the sentimental theme. You will continue to savor your freedom and it will be a period for you to heal the wounds left by past relationships.

Think carefully before trying to start a relationship that does not bring anything positive to your life. By the end of the year, things will change. Maybe a person will arrive who can understand your way of being and you will establish a very good loving relationship. If this happens, do everything you need, but don't hide anything.

If you have a partner you can have a year full of love, the relationship will look to the future, there will be excellent closeness and kindness will inhabit your relationship all year round. There will be situations that will try to damage your relationship, you should not allow them to affect your love life, try to solve them and prevent third parties from taking advantage of this situation.

There will be a lot of independence in your partner, you should take advantage of this, but do not forget to act wisely, remembering that fidelity is important. Try to stay away from people flirting with you and avoid entering an area that can cause headaches.

Success escorts your professional life, but you will have to strive and work hard to achieve it. After

August you will achieve that goal for which you have fought so hard.

This is a good period in the field of finance, although there is a possibility of having some expenses, but when the gale passes, you will enjoy financial peace again. You will be presented with opportunities to have new sources of income; you must be very wise and analyze what your best alternatives are.

With regard to health it is important that you keep anxiety levels to a minimum so that they do not cause difficult situations. You must practice some sport, rest the required hours because this will help you enjoy excellent health.

You will be presented with opportunities to buy a home, and you should take into account your budget and the debt you will acquire.

Your married life will be stable, but you must plan surprise outings so that the flame of love does not die.

New friends will enter your circle of friends, it is important that you use your intuition to know which are real friends and not fake. Remember that we must know people well before trusting them blindly.

Optimism is essential for you to succeed, and so is intuition. You must be very positive in the face of some challenges.

Combination of Zodiac Signs with Chinese Horoscope Signs

When you combine Eastern and Western horoscopes, it is incredible the connection that exists and how correct they are.

Chinese and Western horoscopes are the most used. If you have the possibility to understand them deeply, this will make it easier for you to use them and have a centralized approach.

Both horoscopes are based on the position of the stars, but in the Chinese horoscope 28 constellations are used, and in the western 88. Both agree that they have 12 essential segmentations. The Chinese horoscope is based on 12 animals that rule each year, and the western horoscope on 12 signs that govern each month.

The Chinese Horoscope is based on the lunar calendar and is the oldest known horoscope so far. Your zodiac sign matches your sign in the Chinese horoscope, but that does not happen often. If that were the case, the predictions would be more accurate.

There is an equivalence between the signs of both horoscopes:

Aries/Dragon, Taurus/Snake, Gemini/Horse, Cancer/Goat, Leo/Monkey, Virgo/Rooster, Libra/Dog, Scorpion/Pig, Sagittarius/Rat, Capricorn/Ox, Aquarius/Tiger, and Pisces/Rabbit.

Combinations

Pig

Aries / Pig

A combination that gives exceedingly kind and affable people. They are peaceful from birth; they detest problems and gossip. They avoid conflicts, smell them from a distance. Is optimistic, has excellent mental and emotional health, and ability to work hard

They tend to deceive themselves in sentimental matters, and that is why when they suffer a disappointment they become a meringue. They are generous, they are in constant search of their soulmate and when they find it they give themselves unconditionally.

Taurus / Pig

A mixture that results in very accommodating people. They love to have fun, they are cheerful and have a lot of patience. They are very hardworking and fighting, and kind. Sometimes they are unfriendly when things do not happen as they wish. Their generosity is sometimes harnessed by unscrupulous people.

They are compassionate, methodical, and attuned to their emotions.

Gemini/ Pig

Combination brought to the world by people who are cheerful, but irresponsible. They cannot have obligations because they are overwhelmed.

They always disagree with everyone, and they like to be arguing over insignificant things. They are jealous of their partners, controlling and insecure. Their imagination is strong, they see ghosts where there are none, and their reputation is doubtful.

Cancer/ Pig

Very self-sufficient people. They think they are the navel of the universe, and they like everyone to pay attention to them. They fight for their success, and they love fame.

He is cheerful, and balanced, but very vulnerable to criticism. He has sudden mood swings and is very sincere in expressing his emotions. For them it is essential to have money since they connect their emotional states to this energy.

Leo / Pig
These people are leaders, love the good life and will strive to have the comforts they think they deserve. However, they are very compassionate and kind. They are sensitive to other people's emotions and generous to their family and friends. They know how to control their finances; they can be self-centered and capricious.

They enjoy social and family gatherings where everyone gathers and enjoys their charismatic and attractive presence.

Virgo / Pig
This connection gives reasonable people. They are very discreet, and suspicious. They stand out for their altruism, and if it cannot help you, it will advise you. It becomes an ice stone during

conflicts, and momentarily can if it breaks or accuses you of its ills. They can be pessimistic, and because they receive the support they need, they are prone to states of depression.

They persevere in what they want to achieve, they are honest, and they do not like absurd goals.

Libra/Pig
A combination that stands out for its insight. They never cross boundaries unless they have authorization, either with friends or partners. Brilliant for negotiations, and cautious in their opinions.

He does everything possible not to be involved in conflict situations. He does not stand falsehoods, and traps, and neither do injustices.

Scorpion / Pig
These two signs are typical of people who seem naïve but are highly intelligent. They like to analyze you to know that you can give them benefit. They are selfish, and vain. They have sophisticated strategies to win people's love and friendship. They are charismatic and enjoy when they are the center of attention.

They are planned, they hate the unforeseen, and they go from happiness to sadness very easily.

Sagittarius/Pig
These two signs result in individuals who are compassionate and optimistic. They stand out for their honesty, and their repulsion toxic people. They are people who when they have to say something do speak plainly, they are direct and appreciate that you are equal with them. They place great value on the opinions of others, listen to the advice they receive with gratitude and have an enviable energy.

Everything they propose they achieve because when they have a purpose in it, they put all their energies and focus.

Capricorn / Pig
People with these signs are very relaxed, they go through life without tormenting themselves and know that there is always a second chance. They communicate openly and it is very friendly. They are emotional, they are very pleasant and with them you never get bored at a party, and they always have something to tell.

Their temperament is strong, they are very worthy, you can trust them and tell them a secret they take to the grave.

Aquarius / Pig
This combination exposes a tendency to out-of-this-world logical thinking. In general, they are very balanced people, and their mind is always active to find the best solutions to any conflict situation.

They are kind people who enjoy giving you a hand, always acknowledging their faults and learning from experiences. They are known for having an X-ray eye for any detail, and with this feature they are the right people for jobs that carry this type of skill,

Pisces / Pig
The combination of these signs is typical of people who have many spiritual values. They are peaceful and, in any circumstance, will do everything possible not to get involved in conflicts. They are not selfish and if they have to walk the extra mile for you they will do it without a second thought.

They are workers worthy of admiration, they try their best, even if they are exhausted. They don't stop when they get tired, but when they finish.

The Decoration of your Home according to Feng Shui

Feng Shu is a Chinese philosophy that examines the environment, based on the theory of Yin and Yang, and the Five Elements.

Experts have shown that areas of ancient China were regularly chosen in territories that are surrounded by mountains and had a river. Only was it not because these areas provided the primary criteria to survive, but they did it to follow the patterns established by Feng Shui.

The main idea of Feng Shui is to achieve balance between humanity and the Universe. If there are good energies, there is balance, since Feng Shui affects the destiny of each person.

Through the study of Feng Shui, human beings can work on their compatibility with nature, their environment, and their lives, to achieve more prosperity, and health in life.

Five Elements Theory

The Five Elements theory is a part of Feng Shui. These elements are important to specify the right Feng Shui in each space. These elements are Fire, Earth, Metal, Water and Wood, and each one has a particularity that symbolizes specific aspects of life.

The Five Elements are the expression that Feng Shui uses to explain the structure of nature, and these elements act together and must always be balanced.

Feng Shui for the Twelve Signs of the Chinese Horoscope

Rat

Water favors people who were born under the sign of the Rat, helps them to obtain prosperity. To get plenty they should put a fish tank with goldfish in the northern part of their office.

Ox

People of this sign will achieve prosperity if they use the Fire element. To achieve this, they must put porcelain or ceramic items in their businesses or offices, and in their home.

Tiger

The earth element is the one that should be used by individuals belonging to the sign of the Tiger. They must add something relevant that symbolizes this earth element. A pot with a plant, or a natural flower that grows can bring prosperity to your lives.

Rabbit

To be lucky and attract abundance, people of the Rabbit sign require a secret element of earth in their lives. You should hide a jade or citrine quartz in the northeastern part of your home or office.

Dragon

The Northwest is excellent for those who were born under the sign of the Dragon. In this direction they should put a container with clear water mixed with a little soil. Another choice is to place a Lotus Flower in a bowl.

Snake

Prosperity will come to the lives of individuals belonging to the sign of the Serpent if they use Metal objects, specifically Gold and Silver, in their home or offices.

Horse

The Northwest is the recommended position for people of the sign of the Horse to obtain a large capital. They should put a metal frog in the Northwest of their home or business.

Goat

The North is the appropriate cardinal point for people who were born under the sign of the Goat. They should put a wooden box, or other wooden object, in the north of their offices or home. If they use a wooden box, inside they must put an object related to their profession in it. For example, a writer may place a pencil in the box.

Monkey

For prosperity to come into the lives of people who were born under the sign of the Monkey, they must place in the western part of the house or business, a plant of their size, or larger, in that cardinal point.

Rooster

Good luck will come to the lives of those who belong to the sign of the Rooster, if they place some seeds in a dark red glass, bottle, or bowl. They should not use any metal.

Dog

People who belong to the sign of the Dog should dispense with the elements Water and Earth in their lives. They can put plant trunks or branches in their office or home, but they cannot put it in water or soil.

Pig

People who were born under the sign of the Pig require the Fire element in their lives to bring good luck. They can place a ceramic tray, or other items made of clay in their home offices. Ceramic items are passed through fire for completion.

About the Author

In addition to her astrological knowledge, Alina Rubi has an abundant professional education; She holds certifications in Psychology, Hypnosis, Reiki, Bioenergetic Healing with Crystals, Angelic Healing, Dream Interpretation and is a Spiritual Instructor. She has knowledge of Gemology, which she uses to program stones or minerals and turn them into powerful Amulets or Talismans of protection.

Rubi has a practical and purposeful character, which has allowed it to have a special and integrating vision of several worlds, easing solutions to specific problems. Alina writes the Monthly Horoscopes for the website of the American Association of Astrologers; you can read them on the www.astrologers.com website. At this moment he writes a weekly column in the newspaper El Nuevo Herald on spiritual topics, published every Friday in digital form and on Mondays in print. He also has a program and

*weekly horoscope on the YouTube channel of this
newspaper. His Astrological Yearbook is published
every year in the newspaper "Diario las
Américas", under the column Rubi Astrologa.*

*Rubi has drafted several articles on astrology for
the monthly publication "Today's Astrologer", has
taught Astrology, Tarot, Hand Reading, Crystal
Healing, and Esotericism. He has a weekly video
on astrology topics on the Nuevo Herald YouTube
channel. She had her own astrology program
broadcast daily through Flamingo T.V., has been
interviewed by several TV and radio programs,
and every year her "Astrological Yearbook" is
published with the horoscope sign by sign and
other interesting mystical topics.*

*She is the author of the books "Rice and Beans for
the Soul" Part I, II, and III a compilation of
esoteric articles, published in English and Spanish,
"Money for All Pockets", "Love for All Hearts",
"Health for All Bodies, Astrological Yearbook
2021, Horoscope 2022, Rituals and Spells for
Success in 2022 Spells and Secrets, Astrology,
Rituals and Amulets 2023 and Chinese Horoscope
2023 classes all available in seven languages.*

*It has its YouTube channel with topics of
psychology, esotericism, and astrology, where you
can enjoy videos about soulmates, reincarnation,*

body language, astral travel, the evil eye, spells and many more topics.

Rubi speaks English and Spanish perfectly, combines all her talents and knowledge in her readings. He currently lives in Miami, Florida.

For more information you can visit the website www.esoterismomagia.com

Angeline A. Rubi is the daughter of Alina Rubi. As a child she was interested in all esoteric subjects and practices astrology and Kabbalah from the age of four. He has knowledge of Tarot, Reiki, and Gemology. She is not only the author, but editor of all the books published by her and her mother.

For more information you can contact her by email: rubiediciones29@gmail.com

Printed in Great Britain
by Amazon

26737816R00051